W9-CJL-006

A to Z Italy

BY JUSTINE AND RON FONTES

children's press®

A Division of Scholastic Inc.
New York Toronto London Auckland Sydney
Mexico City New Delhi Hong Kong
Danbury, Connecticut

Series Consultant: Linda D. Bullock, Ph.D.
Series Design: Marie O'Neill
Photo Research: Candlepants Incorporated

The photos on the cover shows bowtie pasta (top), the Leaning Tower of Pisa (right), Italian boys (bottom), and a detail taken from *Creation of Adam*, by Michaelangelo.

Photographs ©2003: Corbis Images: 27 center (AFP), 32 (Austrian Archives), 13 top (David Ball), 28 left (Annie Griffiths Belt), 14 left, 27 bottom, 33 (Bettmann), cover bottom left, 22 left (Jonathan Blair), 17 top (Ed Bohon), 6 left (Derek Croucher), 27 top (Dennis Degnan), 25 bottom (Owen Franken), 5 left, 9 top, 17 bottom (Todd Gipstein), 35 bottom (Kit Houghton), 12 top left (Hulton-Deutsch Collection), 25 top left (Helen King), 4 right (Maurizio Lanini), 8 bottom (Charles & Josette Lenars), 34 bottom (Massimo Listri), 5 right, 13 bottom (Araldo de Luca), 25 top right (William Manning), 14 right (Doug Mazell), 29 (John and Lisa Merrill), 15 bottom (Gianni Dagli Orti), 4 left (Stan Osolinski), 15 top (Studio Patellani), 8 top (Vittoriano Rastelli), 12 top right (Nicolas Sapieha), 28 right (TempSport), 16 bottom (Sandro Vannini), cover top left (World Films Enterprise), 30 (Michael S. Yamashita), 16 top (Bo Zaunders); Corbis Sygma/Origlia Franco: 12 bottom; Envision Stock Photography Inc.: 9 bottom (Curzon Studio), 38 (Rita Maas), 11 left (Steven Mark Needham), 11 right (Zeva Oelbaum); MapQuest.com, Inc.: 21; PictureQuest/Steve Allen/Brand X Pictures: cover bottom right; SODA/Photodisc: cover top; Stone/Getty Images: 34 top (Nello Giambi), 10 top (Martyn Goddard), 7, 22 right, 23 (Simeone Huber), 31 (Trevor Wood); The Image Bank/Getty Images: 18, 19 (Grant V. Faint), 24 (Andrea Pistolesi), 10 bottom (Stefano Scata), 6 right (Harald Sund); The Image Works: 36, 37 left, 37 right (Yashiro Haga), 35 top (Pinnizzotto/Imapress), 26 (Topham).
Map by XNR Productions

Library of Congress Cataloging-in-Publication Data
Fontes, Justine.
  Italy / by Justine and Ron Fontes.
       p. cm. – (A-Z)
Includes index. Audience: "Ages 7-9". Contents: Animals – Buildings – Cities – Dress – Exports – Food – Government – History – Important people – Jobs – Keepsakes– Land – Map – Nation – Only in Italy – People – Question – Religion – School and sports – Transportation – Unusual places – Visiting the country – Window to the past – X-tra special things – Yearly festivals – Zuppa – Let's explore more – Meet the authors –
Italian and English words you know.
  ISBN 0-516-24559-7 (lib. bdg.)   0-516-26812-0 (pbk.)
1. Italy–Juvenile literature. [1. Italy. 2. Alphabet.] I. Fontes, Ron. II. Title. III. Series.
  DS706.K67 2003
  [E] –dc21
                                        2003003702

■ Contents

chamois

Lupo

(LOO-poh)
means wolf.

The wolf used to be a symbol
of Rome, Italy's capital.

You'll see cats all over Italy. They find cozy places to nap, like this red-tiled roof.

This is one of the statues of Romulus and Remus's wolf mother.

Animals

One animal you'll find in Italy is the wolf. Long ago, people told stories about twin brothers named Romulus and Remus. The stories say that a wolf raised them after their mother died. The brothers grew up and started the city of Rome.

The **chamois** (SHAM-ee) lives here too. It is a goatlike animal that lives in the mountains. It climbs steep mountains and leaps across wide spaces. It can leap up to 40 feet (12 m).

A beautiful fountain shaped like a boat sits at the bottom of the Spanish Steps.

Buildings

Did you know there is an eight-story tower in Italy that has been leaning for hundreds of years? It is called the Leaning Tower of Pisa. Scientists are working hard to keep it from falling over. It leans because the soil moves beneath it. It also contains 28,000 pounds (12,700 kg) of marble. No wonder it's sinking!

There are other beautiful buildings in Italy. A few surround the Spanish Steps in Rome. Long ago, people who worked for the Spanish government lived here.

Cities

Vaporétto

(vah-poh-REH-toh)
is a waterbus.

Venice is built on 117 islands. You won't find cars or buses there. Waterbuses carry people on the canals, or narrow waterways, that flow between the islands.

The Grand Canal is Venice's main street. For hundreds of years, rich families built palaces along the canal.

Some people like to see the palaces while riding in small boats called **gondolas**. The people who guide the boats are called **gondoliers**.

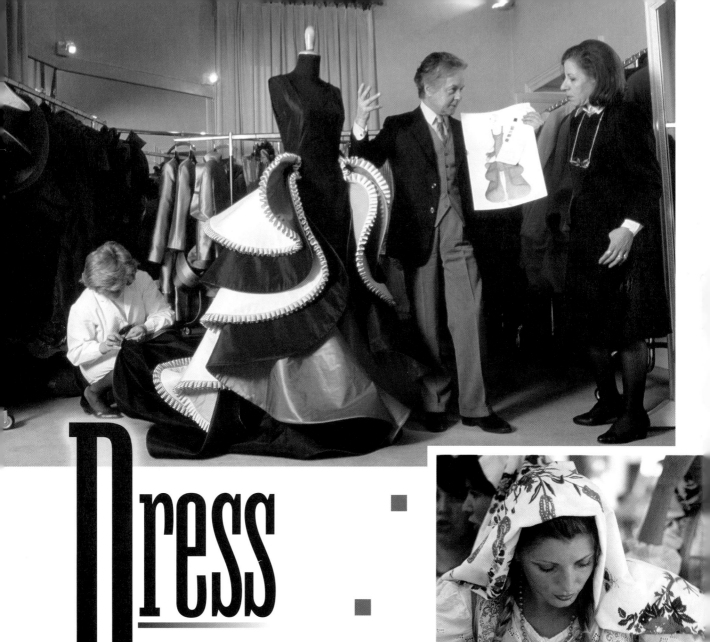

Dress

There are lots of reasons to dress up in Italy. On special holidays, some people wear costumes from long ago.

Children often wear shorts and t-shirts. Adults who work in cities wear suits and shoes made from fine materials.

People from around the world come to Italy to visit cities like Milan. In Milan, there are shops that sell some of the most beautiful clothing in the world.

A Swiss Guard stands in colorful uniform outside the Vatican, where the Pope lives.

Ferrari sports cars are famous for being fast and beautiful.

Exports

Bicycles, motor scooters, and cars come from Italy. Many foods we eat like fruits, vegetables, wines, cheeses, and olive oil are also important exports.

Much of the world's marble comes from **quarries** in Italy. Quarries are large pits where workers dig out the stone. Some of the most famous marble comes from quarries near the town of Carrara.

Italian artists sell statues made from marble. They also sell glass that is blown by hand, lace, and jewelry.

Italian Salad Dressing Recipe

WHAT YOU NEED:
- 1 cup extra virgin olive oil
- 1/4 cup white wine vinegar
- 2 tablespoons lemon juice
- 1 teaspoon of salt
- 1 teaspoon of sugar
- 1/2 teaspoon each of pepper, dry mustard, and oregano
- 1/4 teaspoon each of paprika and basil

HOW TO MAKE IT:
Put everything in a jar with a tight lid. Shake well before serving.

Food

Italians use olive oil on many foods, including salads. Ask an adult to help you make some Italian salad dressing using the recipe above.

The Italian Parliament meets in Rome.

Alcide de Gasperi (right) was Italy's prime minister from 1945 to 1953.

Government

Italy is a republic. In a republic, voters choose people to speak for them in government. Italy used to have a king, but people wanted a republic. Italians celebrate the day their government changed. They call it **Republic Day**.

The president chooses a prime minister. A prime minister is the head of the **parliament**. The parliament makes laws for the country. Voters choose most of the people in the parliament.

Today, **Silvio Berlusconi** is Italy's prime minister.

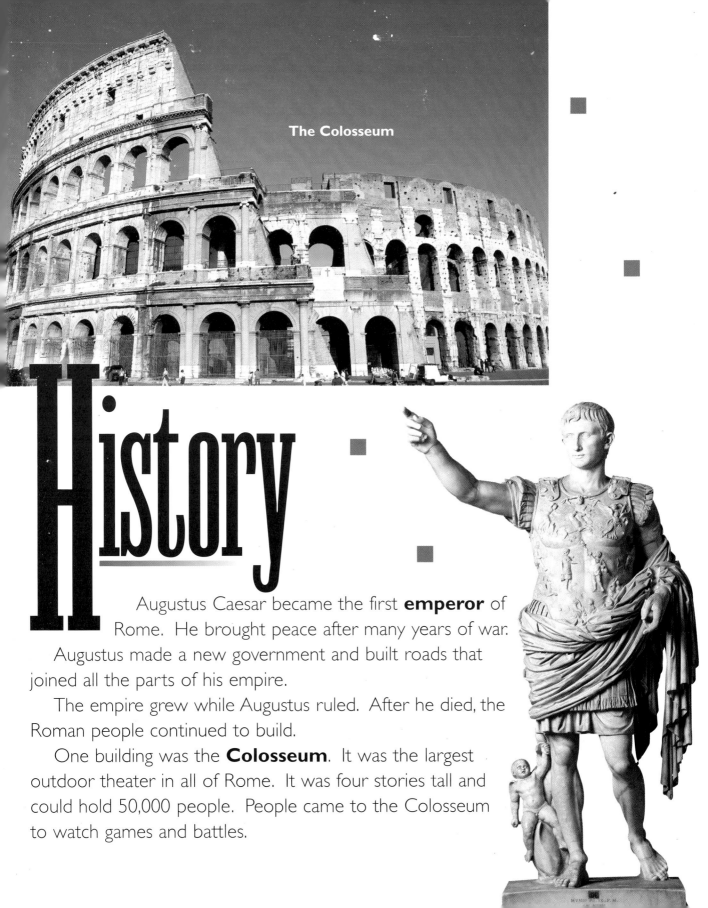

The Colosseum

History

Augustus Caesar became the first **emperor** of Rome. He brought peace after many years of war. Augustus made a new government and built roads that joined all the parts of his empire.

The empire grew while Augustus ruled. After he died, the Roman people continued to build.

One building was the **Colosseum**. It was the largest outdoor theater in all of Rome. It was four stories tall and could hold 50,000 people. People came to the Colosseum to watch games and battles.

Important People

Many of the world's greatest painters, builders, musicians, actors, and writers are Italian.

People have been listening to opera singers at "La Scala," opera house in Milan, Italy, since 1778.

Leonardo Da Vinci

Sophia Loren is a great Italian actress. She made films in Italy and the United States.

Pastello

(pah-STEH-loh)
is a crayon.

Leonardo Da Vinci was an artist and a scientist. He made great paintings and drew plans for amazing machines.

He was born near Florence in 1452. He painted two of the most famous paintings in the world. They are named *The Mona Lisa* and *The Last Supper*.

Da Vinci also dreamed of flying machines. He thought about them long before people believed they could work. He had even drawn plans for a helicopter!

The Mona Lisa

15

Jobs

There are many different kinds of jobs in Italy. A chef is one of them. They cook in restaurants and teach in cooking schools all over the world.

Another interesting job is a conservator. This person is responsible for taking care of museum and other artifacts. They repair these ancient materials to preserve history.

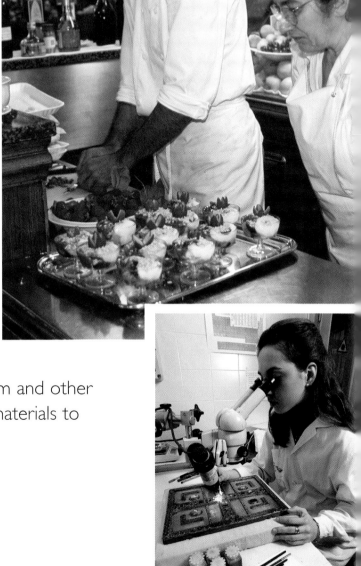

This woman is using a microscope to repair this 6th century book cover.

Spaghetti
(spah-GEH-tee)
You probably already know the Italian word spaghetti. Yum!

Many Italian masks look like animal faces.

Keepsakes

Gondoliers dress in striped sailor shirts and straw hats with ribbons, like this one.

Each year, Italians celebrate Carnevale. The holiday lasts one month. People go to parties dressed in fancy costumes. They also wear beautiful masks. You can buy these masks from shops all year long.

Land

Italy is shaped like a boot. It is a peninsula. That means it has water on three sides.

Italy has beautiful hills and mountains. The Alps run across northern Italy. They divide Italy from the rest of Europe. The Apennine Mountains run all the way down the country, like a zipper on a boot.

Italy has islands, too. The biggest island is Sicily. It sits near the toe of the boot. The second largest island is Sardinia.

There are two small countries in Italy. The Republic of San Marino which is near Florence, and **Vatican City**, which is in Rome.

Montagna
(mone-TAHG-nah)
means mountain.

Nation

Italy's flag is green, white, and red. Italians first used the flag in 1796. They wanted it to show their support for a French emperor named Napoleon. Napoleon's favorite color was green, so he gave the flag a green stripe. White and red were the same as the colors on the French flag.

In 1946, Italy became a republic. The new country chose the three-colored flag as its own.

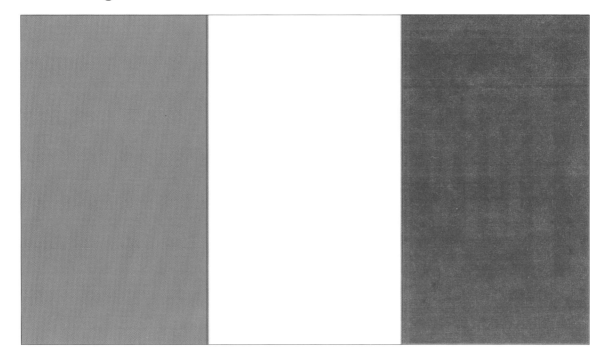

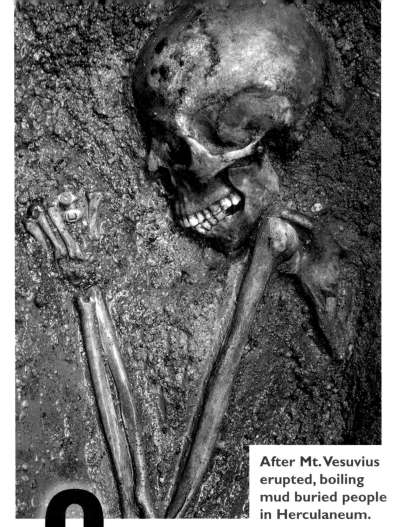

After Mt. Vesuvius erupted, boiling mud buried people in Herculaneum.

Only in Italy

Mt. Vesuvius is a **volcano**. In A.D. 79, it erupted, or exploded. Hot, melted rock called lava spilled out of the volcano.

Only in Siena, twice each summer, there is a horse race. Riders wear costumes like those worn hundreds of years ago. People from around the world come to cheer.

Lava and mud from Mt. Vesuvius buried nearby towns like Herculaneum. Pompeii was also buried.

Hot ashes and bits of stone rained on Pompeii. Poisonous gases from the volcano filled the air. The poisonous air killed many people and animals. Their bodies were buried under tons of ash. Over time, their bodies broke down. Only holes were left in the ash. Scientists poured plaster into the holes. When the plaster hardened, scientists could see statues of the people and animals that once lived in Pompeii.

Scheletro

(skeh-LEH-trroh)
means skeleton.

23

These homes are in Venice.

People

Italian families are very close. Children often live at home until they are married. After they marry, most people stay close to their families. They visit often and share holidays.

In Tuscany, many homes are two story brick or stone buildings.

Italy has many regions. People in each region may speak a different form of Italian. They also have their own kinds of cooking. Even their towns and buildings look different.

25

Pizza is the Italian word for pie.

Question

Who invented pizza?

Did you know that **pizza** was invented in Italy in 1889? Raffaele Esposito, a baker, baked a special pizza for the king and queen's visit to Naples. The baker used flat bread and put red tomatoes, white mozzarella cheese, and green basil on top. These were the colors of Italy.

Italians who moved to the United States brought the idea of pizza with them. When American soldiers came back from Europe after World War II, they knew about pizza, too. Now people all over America eat pizza!

The Pope's official church is St. Peter's Basilica in Vatican City.

Religion

Pope John Paul II leads the Catholic church today.

Mother Cabrini

Almost all Italians are Roman Catholics. The head of the Roman Catholic Church is called the **pope**.

In 1946, the Roman Catholic Church made Marie Francis Cabrini a saint. Mother Cabrini had grown up on a farm in Italy. She wanted to be a **missionary**. Marie helped start and run schools, children's homes, and hospitals around the world. In 1909, she became a citizen of the United States.

Azzurri

(ah-SOO-ree)
Soccer players wear
blue uniforms.
Azzurro means blue,
so the players are
called azzurri.

School & Sports

All Italian children from ages 6 to 14 go to school. At 14, students choose what to study. Some stay in school to learn more science, history, language, and art. Others go to special schools that teach them how to use computers.

Summer is soccer time in Italy. Many begin to play when they are children. Italians also swim, play water polo, and cycle. Some do lawn bowling called bocce.

Transportation

Cars and taxis zip along Italy's highways and narrow city streets. Some riders prefer to ride motor scooters and motorcycles.

People can also move around the country by train. The fastest train is the modern Eurostar.

Italy's airline is called Alitalia. Airplanes are only one way to reach Italy's beautiful islands.

Ferries also carry people across the seas around Italy, including the Mediterranean Sea.

Unusual Places

Long ago, the Orsini family lived at their **villa** near a town called Bomarzo. When Mr. Orsini's wife died, he built a park for her. The park is unusual. There are trees and deer, but there is more. He hired an artist to sculpt a garden of monsters! There are also buildings that were built to look as though they are falling down.

This head and hand were once part of a giant statue of a Roman emperor.

Visiting the Country

The pope asked Michelangelo to design, or draw plans, for an ancient hill in Rome. The artist's plans included two palaces. Today, the palaces are museums, like the one above. They hold many paintings and sculptures.

Michelangelo also produced great art. In Florence, there is a 17-foot tall statue of David, a hero from the Bible. The artist Michelangelo sculpted David from marble. He also painted Bible stories on the ceiling of the Sistine Chapel in Vatican City.

Window to the Past

People have been making wine for about 5,000 years. Wine comes from the juice of crushed grapes.

(above) These workers are resting from grape picking. The grapes they pick may be used to make a famous Italian wine called *Chianti* (kee-AHN-tee.)

Before modern times, Italians did many chores by hand. Some people carried firewood on their backs and used animals to help them farm.

Wine is a part of Italian culture. People in different regions of Italy grow different kinds of grapes that make different kinds of wines.

First the grapes are picked then a machine removes the stem from the grape. The grapes pass through a press to get the juice out.

The grape juice is **fermented**. Sometimes it takes many years to make good wine. Once the wine has aged, it can be put in a bottle.

You can also visit Vatican City and climb the staircase to one of the Vatican museums.

This is a vase shaped like a human head. The Truscans used vases like this to hold the ashes of dead people.

X-tra Special Things

Carnevale has been celebrated for a long time. People wear unusual and colorful costumes to parades and parties.

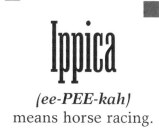

In Italy, you can see the Roman chariots that were driven long ago. Emperors used to hold chariot races. Their drivers drove wooden carts pulled by horses. This was dangerous and people didn't always follow the rules.

Ippica

(ee-PEE-kah)
means horse racing.

Yearly Festivals

Many Italian celebrations are church holidays. Carnevale ends before Lent, a time when Roman Catholics do not eat meat.

Many people like to watch colorful Carnevale floats.

During Carnevale, people eat, drink, and enjoy themselves. They go to parties, balls, and parades in places like Venice and Viareggio.

Each June, there is the flower Festival in Genzano. A city street is divided into 13 parts. A flower master takes charge of each part, using flowers to make pictures and patterns.

There are other kinds of festivals, too. Some celebrate nature. Others tell stories from Italy's long history.

Almost one and a half million flowers are used to make the street carpet for the Flowers Festival.

Vegetale

(vej-uh-TAH-leh)
means plant or vegetable.

This is *minestrone* soup. Minestrone means "hodgepodge." A hodge-podge is a jumble or mix of different things.

Zuppa

Zuppa means soup. Italians often eat soup instead of **pasta** or rice. Sometimes, they also enjoy soup as a light supper.

When people first began eating soup, they used vegetables and beans. Sometimes they added meat.

Today, you can eat many kinds of soup in Italy. There are pasta soups, fish soups, and creamy soups filled with vegetables like zucchini and artichokes. Of course, there is **minestrone**, too. That's a soup filled with vegetables.

Italian and English Words

azzurri (ah-SOO-hee) the blue-uniformed players of Italy's soccer team

azzurro the Italian word for blue

chamois a goatlike deer or the soft leather made from its skin

Colosseum (kaw-luh-SEE-uhm) a huge, round theater built in Rome in A.D. 79

emperor (EM-pur-ur) the ruler of a group of countries, like the Roman Empire

Etruscans (i-TRUS-kuhns) the people who lived in Italy before the Ancient Romans

fermented sugar from grapes goes though a process to become wine

gondola (GON-duh-luh) a slim boat with high, pointed ends and one oar

gondolier (gawn-duh-LER) the person who operates a gondola

ippica (ee-PEE-kah) the Italian word for horse racing

lupo (LOO-poh) the Italian word for wolf

minestrone (mi-nuh-STRONE) the Italian word for hodgepodge

missionary (MISH-uh-ner-ee) a person sent by a church to a foreign country to preach and do good works

montagna (mone-TAHG-nah) the Italian word for mountain

opera (OP-uh-ruh) a play set to music for singers and instruments

parliament (PAR-luh-muhnt) the group of people chosen to make laws for a country

pastello (pah-STEH-loh) the Italian word for crayon

pizza the Italian word for pie

Pope (pohp) the head of the Roman Catholic church

pasta (PAH-stuh) a food made from flour and water molded and cut into various shapes

quarry (KWOR-ee) a place where stone is taken from the ground

Republic Day (ri-PUHB-lik day) the anniversary of June 2, 1946, when Italians gained a government elected by the people

scheletro (skeh-LEH-trroh) the Italian word for skeleton

spaghetti (spah-GEH-tee) long, thin strands of pasta cooked in boiling water

vaporetto (vah-poh-REH-toh) a waterbus

Vatican City the independent country in Rome where the Pope lives

vegetale (vej-uh-TAH-leh) the Italian word for plant or vegetable

villa (VIL-uh) a large country house

volcano (vol-KAY-noh) a mountain with openings in the Earth's crust through which molten rock, ash, and gases sometimes erupt

zuppa the Italian word for soup

Let's Explore More

A Visit To Italy by Rachael Bell, Heinemann Library, 1999

Pompeii Buried Alive by Edith Kunhardt, Bt Bound, 1999

Websites

www.pbs.org/wgbh/nova/pisa
This website includes more information on the Leaning Tower of Pisa and what's being done to prevent it from falling.

www.supersurf.com
Learn more about Italy's people and history.

www.touritaly.org/pompeii/pompeii-main.htm
Learn more about Pompeii by taking the photo tour on this website.

Index

Italic page numbers indicate illustrations.

Meet the Authors

JUSTINE & RON FONTES have written nearly 400 children's books together. Since 1988, they have published *critter news*, a free newsletter that keeps them in touch with publishers from their home in Maine.

The Fonteses have written many biographies and early readers, as well as historical novels and other books combining facts with stories. Their love of animals is expressed in the nature notes columns of *critter news*.

During his childhood in Tennessee, Ron was a member of the Junior Classical League and went on to tutor Latin students. At 16, Ron was drawing a science fiction comic strip for the local newspaper. A professional artist for 30 years, Ron has also been in theater as a costumer, makeup artist, and designer.

Justine was born in New York City and worked in publishing while earning a BA in English Literature Phi Beta Kappa from New York University. Thanks to her parents' love of travel, Justine visited most of Europe as a child, going as far north as Finland. During college, she spent time in France and Spain.